The
SMALL and MIGHTY
Book of
Myths and
Legends

Published in 2023 by OH!.
An imprint of Welbeck Children's Limited, part of Welbeck Publishing Group
Based in London and Sydney.

www.welbeckpublishing.com

Design and layout © Welbeck Children's Limited 2023
Text copyright © Welbeck Children's Limited 2023

A CIP catalogue record for this book is available from the British Library.

Writer: Clive Gifford
Illustrator: Isabel Muñoz
Consultant: Neil Philip
Design and editorial by Raspberry Books Ltd
Editorial Manager: Tash Mosheim
Design Manager: Russell Porter
Production: Jess Brisley

ISBN 978 1 80069 463 7

Printed in Heshan, China

10 9 8 7 6 5 4 3 2 1

FSC
www.fsc.org
MIX
Paper | Supporting
responsible forestry
FSC® C020056

The
SMALL and MIGHTY
Book of
Myths and Legends

Clive Gifford and Isabel Muñoz

Contents

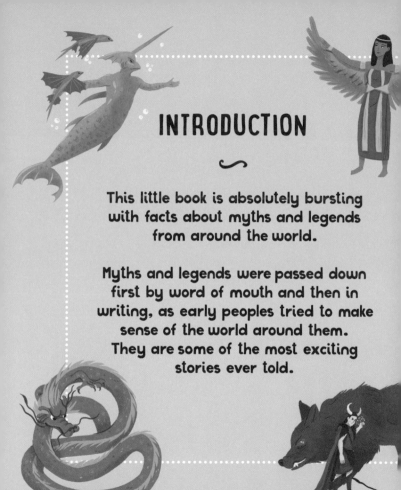

INTRODUCTION

This little book is absolutely bursting with facts about myths and legends from around the world.

Myths and legends were passed down first by word of mouth and then in writing, as early peoples tried to make sense of the world around them. They are some of the most exciting stories ever told.

You will discover . . .

- A three-headed guard dog
- A terrifying sea monster
- A crab monster that kills people by eating their shadows
- How the world was formed from colored clouds

. . . and lots more.

These myths and legends continue to entertain us to this day. Read on and be amazed.

Ancient Greek and Roman Myths

The most
important ancient
Greek gods were called

OLYMPIANS

because it was thought
they all lived on

MOUNT OLYMPUS,

the highest peak in Greece.

∽

At Olympus, the gods drank nectar and enjoyed
music played by the god of music, Apollo,
using a stringed instrument called a lyre.

The gods also quarreled
with each other.

ZEUS

WAS THE RULER OF THE GODS.

BESIDES ZEUS,
THE 12 MOST IMPORTANT
OLYMPIANS WERE:

1. Aphrodite
2. Apollo
3. Ares
4. Artemis
5. Athena
6. Demeter

7. Dionysus
8. Hephaestus
9. Hera
10. Hermes
11. Hestia
12. Poseidon

In Greek myth,

Prometheus

stole the secret of fire from the
gods and gave it to humans.
He was punished by the
gods by being chained to
a rock while an eagle
attacked him for thousands
of years.

Among the first creatures to live in Greek mythology were **Hundred-Handed Giants** who guarded the Underworld, where the souls of people went after they died.

Cerberus

was a three-headed dog who guarded the gates to the Underworld.

Snake heads grew from its back, and it had the tail of a serpent.

Greek philosopher
Plato
told of a giant flood sent
by the gods to punish
the people of Atlantis.
The flood sank their
island beneath the sea.

In Greek myth, **THE TITANS**, led by **ATLAS**, fought the Olympian gods in a ten-year-long series of battles. The Olympians won and Zeus punished Atlas by forcing him to hold up the sky forever.

According to Greek myth,

JASON

persuaded many of Greece's
greatest heroes, including Heracles,
Peleus, and Orpheus, to join him
on a ship he built called the Argo.
This group of heroes, called **the
Argonauts**, battled many
obstacles on their quest.

~

The Argonauts were attacked
by **Harpies**—bird-like beasts
with the heads of women.

In Greek legend,

DAEDALUS

made wings for himself and his son Icarus that allowed them to fly. When Icarus flew too close to the Sun, the wax that held the wings together melted, and he fell to his death.

Persephone

was unhappy living with
Pluto, the Greek god of
the Underworld. A deal was
struck, and she spent six months
each year with her mother,
the farming goddess Demeter,
which gave us SPRING
and SUMMER. For the
other six months, we have
FALL and WINTER.

The ancient Greek hero **Heracles** completed 12 seemingly impossible tasks, called labors. These included killing man-eating birds and **the Hydra,** a nine-headed serpent.

In Greek mythology, the **Chimera** was a fire-breathing monster that was part lion, part goat, and part snake.

THE GREEK HERO **THESEUS** VENTURED THROUGH AN UNDERGROUND **LABYRINTH** ON CRETE TO SLAY THE **MINOTAUR**—A FEARSOME MONSTER WITH THE BODY OF A MAN AND THE HEAD OF A BULL.

THE **LABYRINTH**, DESIGNED BY DAEDALUS, WAS SAID TO BE IMPOSSIBLE TO NAVIGATE, BUT THESEUS UNWOUND **A BALL OF THREAD** AS HE ENTERED TO FIND HIS WAY OUT AGAIN.

In Greek legend, SCYLLA,
a six-headed monster, and CHARYBDIS,
a gigantic whirlpool, wrecked ships
that sailed too close.

The ancient Romans copied many of the Greek gods. The Roman god of transportation and trade, named **Mercury**, was based on the ancient Greek messenger god, **Hermes.**

NEPTUNE was the Roman god of the sea and very similar to the ancient Greek god Poseidon. **He carried a three-pronged spear called a TRIDENT** in one hand and often rode a chariot pulled by sea creatures.

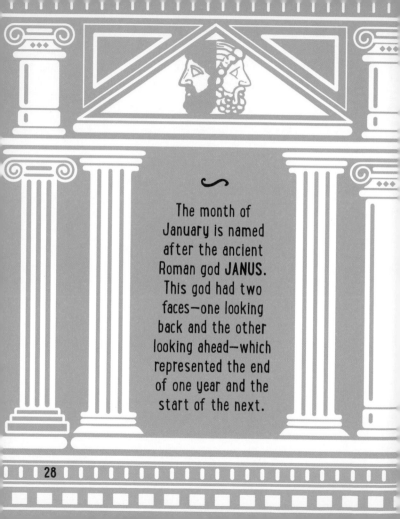

The month of
January is named
after the ancient
Roman god **JANUS**.
This god had two
faces—one looking
back and the other
looking ahead—which
represented the end
of one year and the
start of the next.

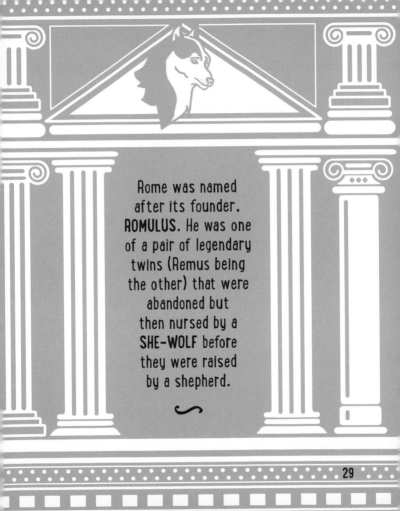

Rome was named after its founder, **ROMULUS**. He was one of a pair of legendary twins (Remus being the other) that were abandoned but then nursed by a **SHE-WOLF** before they were raised by a shepherd.

～ Minerva ～

was the Roman goddess of wisdom and craft. She watched over schoolchildren and craftspeople, such as carpenters and stonemasons.

VENUS was the Roman goddess of love and beauty.

Her son, **CUPID**, had a magical bow and set of arrows. Anyone struck by one of his arrows would fall in love.

∾ DIANA ∾

was the ancient Roman
goddess of wild places
and the Moon.

She was often shown as
a huntress with a bow
and a quiver full
of arrows.

We get the word **Volcano** from **Vulcan**, the ancient Roman god of fire and blacksmiths.

33

Saturnalia

was a Roman festival held every December to celebrate Saturn, the Roman god of growing crops. During the festival, servants and their masters swapped places.

35

Myths from Africa

One of the
most important
mythical figures
in ancient Egypt was

RA, THE SUN GOD.

He was said to sail across the sky
each day in his boat.

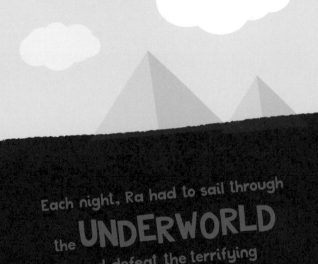

Each night, Ra had to sail through

the **UNDERWORLD**

and defeat the terrifying

GOD OF DARKNESS, APEP.

Ra had to succeed each night
so that he could rise high in
the sky the next day.

~ ANUBIS ~

was an Egyptian god of the dead.
He had the head of a jackal and the
body of a man and helped prepare
dead people for their journey
into the afterlife.

In ancient Egypt, people were often buried with their possessions. Important people were sometimes buried with models of servants called **USHABTIS** to serve them in the afterlife.

In Egyptian myth,
a dead person's heart would be
weighed on scales against the
Feather of Truth held by
the goddess Ma'at.
This showed whether the
person had lived a good,
honest life.

If a person's heart failed the test, it was **DEVOURED** by a monster named Ammut that was part lion, part hippo, and part crocodile.

The Egyptian goddess **Isis** brought her husband, **Osiris**, back to life after he was cut into pieces by his own brother, **Seth**.

Isis put Osiris back together and **fanned her wings** to breathe new life back into him.

Isis and Osiris's son,

HORUS,

was the god of the sky
and was shown with the
the head of a falcon.

Ancient Egyptian
pharaohs believed they
were all descended
from Horus.

～ THOTH ～

WAS THE ANCIENT EGYPTIAN GOD OF WRITING AND WISDOM.

He was usually shown in the form of a baboon and was said to pass on magic and spells to the other Egyptian gods.

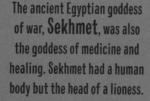

The ancient Egyptian goddess of war, **Sekhmet**, was also the goddess of medicine and healing. Sekhmet had a human body but the head of a lioness.

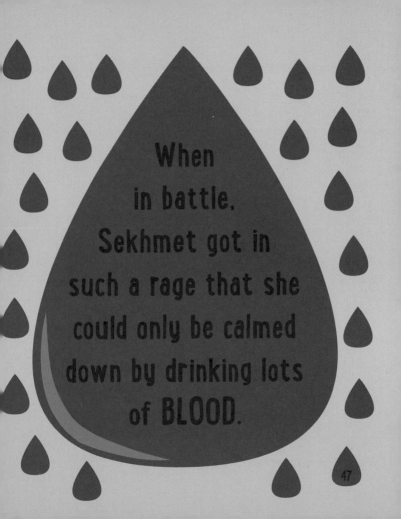

When in battle, Sekhmet got in such a rage that she could only be calmed down by drinking lots of BLOOD.

47

UGANDAN MYTHOLOGY TELLS
HOW **SICKNESS** AND **DEATH**
CAME TO EARTH.

NAMBI lived in heaven
with her father ,**GULU**, the creator.
Nambi fell in love with **KINTU**, the first human.
On a trip to Earth, Nambi was followed by her
brother, **WALUMBE**. Walumbe's name means
"the bringer of sickness and death," and that is
what he brought to Earth.

The Nkala

was a crab monster

in Zambian mythology

that

KILLED

people

by eating

their

shadows.

In the
Congo creation myth,

BUMBA

created the universe
because he was lonely
and unwell.

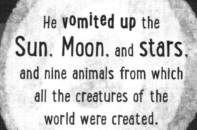

He **vomited up** the
Sun, Moon, and stars,
and nine animals from which
all the creatures of the
world were created.

In West African folklore,

the **NINKI NANKA**

is a fantastical beast with the
head of a horse, the body
of a crocodile, and a long neck
like a giraffe's.

THE NINKI NANKA LIVES IN RIVERS ...

The only thing that the fearsome creature is afraid of is its own reflection, so people carry mirrors for protection.

... AND CAUSES DISEASE AND DEATH. 53

THERE ARE MANY RIVER
GODS AND SPIRITS IN
AFRICAN MYTHOLOGY.

∾

THE **JENGU** IS A
RIVER SPIRIT, OFTEN SHOWN
AS A MERMAID, WHO BRINGS
PEOPLE GOOD LUCK.

MOKELE-MBEMBE

HAS THE POWER TO STOP
RIVERS FROM FLOWING.

∽

THE CREATURE HAS A UNICORN'S
HEAD ON A FOUR-LEGGED LIZARD
BODY AND LOOKS LIKE
A DINOSAUR. SOME PEOPLE CLAIM
IT IS A REAL CREATURE THAT
LIVES IN THE CONGO.

IN THE **YORUBA** RELIGION IN NIGERIA, **SHANGO** IS A POWERFUL EARTH GOD.

HE IS SAID TO BREATHE IN A MAGIC RED POWDER TO CREATE FIRE, WITH WHICH HE BURNS TREES AND VILLAGES.

Biloko are hairless trolls that protect forests in the Democratic Republic of the Congo. They can put spells on anyone they come across and open their mouths so wide they can swallow a human whole.

In Ethiopian myth,

all blacksmiths were considered
to possess magical powers.

For example, they could turn into hyenas
that could eat people.

ACCORDING TO THE KAMBA TRIBE OF KENYA, ELEPHANTS WERE CREATED when one woman applied a magic potion to her teeth to make them grow longer.

She eventually grew GIANT tusks and a thick skin and gave birth to the first elephant herd.

59

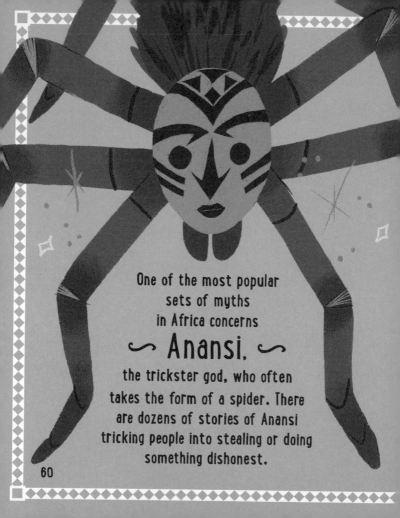

One of the most popular
sets of myths
in Africa concerns
Anansi,
the trickster god, who often
takes the form of a spider. There
are dozens of stories of Anansi
tricking people into stealing or doing
something dishonest.

IN ONE STORY, ANANSI TRIES TO STEAL ALL THE WORLD'S KNOWLEDGE, GATHERING IT INTO A GOURD OR POT. HE ENDS UP THROWING ALL THE KNOWLEDGE INTO THE WIND. THIS IS HOW WISDOM WAS SCATTERED ALL AROUND THE WORLD.

In West African myth,

EsHu

is the god of chaos and confusion who stands at

crossroads and sends people in the wrong direction.

62

IT'S SAID THAT ESHU
PERSUADED THE SUN
AND MOON TO CHANGE
PLACES, GIVING US
NIGHT AND DAY.

63

European Myths

A mysterious pied piper (dressed like a magpie in black and white) played a tune to rid the German town of Hamelin of all its rats.

When the townspeople refused to pay him.

the piper returned.

played again ...

...and led the town's children away.

Anjanas

are good fairies in Spanish folklore who help injured or lost people and animals in forests. They are said to measure just 6 in tall and often leave gifts at the doors of kind people.

In Slavic mythology, **SVAROG**, king of the gods, worked as a blacksmith to create new gods.

These joined him to defeat a giant **black serpent** named Czernobog from taking over the world.

A long Old English poem tells how a young warrior named **BEOWULF** managed to slay a hideous monster called **GRENDEL** who terrorized an ancient kingdom in the country that is now Denmark.

In English folklore,
Jenny Greenteeth
was a river witch with green skin
who lived underwater. She would
catch and eat any children who
strayed too close to the water.

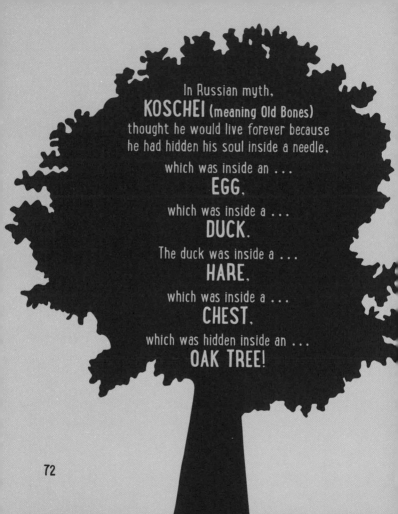

In Russian myth,
KOSCHEI (meaning Old Bones)
thought he would live forever because
he had hidden his soul inside a needle,

which was inside an ...
EGG,

which was inside a ...
DUCK.

The duck was inside a ...
HARE,

which was inside a ...
CHEST,

which was hidden inside an ...
OAK TREE!

72

Marya Morevna

was a BRAVE WARRIOR QUEEN
who managed to kill Koschei
in order to rescue her
husband, Ivan.

According to the myth, she
burned Koschei's body so he
could not live forever.

A legendary creature of central Europe, the **Tatzelwurm** had the head and body of a wildcat and a reptile's long tail.

THE TATZELWURM WAS SAID TO LIVE BENEATH THE ALPS.

LOU CARCOLH was a gruesome giant snail with a serpent's head from French folklore. It was said to use its long, hairy tentacles as whips to injure people.

75

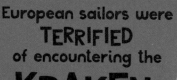

European sailors were **TERRIFIED** of encountering the **KRAKEN.**

This **GIANT,** legendary sea monster could pull entire ships below the water with its many powerful arms. It may have been based on sightings of real-life giant squid.

More than a thousand
sightings are claimed of a
MYSTERIOUS PREHISTORIC

MONSTER

swimming in the
Scottish lake of LOCH NESS.

༄

These stem back over 1,000 years,
from the first possible mention in the
500s CE of an encounter between Saint
Columba and the monster.

THE MORRIGAN was the Irish goddess of war who could change shape from a beautiful woman to become a **RAVEN**.

She hovered over battlefields and influenced the outcome of wars.

TÍR NA NÓG is a mythical land in Celtic folklore where everyone is young and there is no pain or suffering, just joy and beauty.

According to Irish legend, the **GIANT'S CAUSEWAY** . . .

. . . was created by the giant **FIONN MAC CUMHAILL** (also known as Finn McCool).

He was said to have TORN UP ROCK to form a bridge across the Irish Sea so he could battle a Scottish giant.

In English folklore, **Arthur** became king when only he could remove a sword from a block of stone. When this sword was damaged in a duel, a lady of the lake handed him a new sword called . . .

. . . EXCALIBUR.

Arthur met with his loyal knights in his castle, CAMELOT, at a round table. Arthur's knights set off on a perilous quest to find the HOLY GRAIL—a sacred relic of JESUS CHRIST, who Christians believe is the SON OF GOD.

Three knights—Bors, Perceval, and Galahad—were successful.

WE GET THE WORD
'WEDNESDAY' FROM
'WODEN'S DAY.' WODEN
WAS THE OLD ENGLISH
NAME FOR THE
SCANDINAVIAN GOD
ODIN.

ODIN WAS THE LEADER OF THE SCANDINAVIAN GODS WHO LIVED IN **ASGARD.** HE IS SAID TO HAVE EXCHANGED ONE OF HIS EYES IN RETURN FOR RECEIVING ALL THE WISDOM OF THE WORLD.

THOR
was the Scandinavian god
of THUNDER and
LIGHTNING.

He wielded a mighty hammer called **Mjölnir**, which could smash a mountain in a single strike.

Mjölnir always returned to Thor's hand whenever it was thrown.

85

The Vikings believed that half of those who died in battle were taken by winged women called **Valkyries** to Valhalla in Odin's service. Valhalla was a hall in Asgard, the land of the Scandinavian gods. The other half were claimed by the goddess Freyja.

Those who didn't die in battle **WENT TO HEL,** presided over by a **gloomy goddess** also called **Hel.**

AT VALHALLA,

THE FALLEN VIKING WARRIORS
SPENT EVERY DAY FIGHTING
AND EVERY NIGHT FEASTING
WHILE THEIR WOUNDS HEALED
MIRACULOUSLY.

∽

The warriors were
supplied with unlimited
drinks by a giant goat
named Heidrun that lived
on the hall's roof.

In Scandinavian myths, Midgard and Asgard were joined by a **rainbow bridge** called **Bifrost**, which allowed the gods to visit humans. The rainbow was guarded by a watcher god called **Heimdall**.

LOKI was a mischievous god in Scandinavian mythology. He tricked another god, Baldr, into being killed by a piece of mistletoe.

Ragnarök is a series of events that ends the world in Scandinavian mythology. In one of the first events to occur, the Sun and Moon are eaten by two giant wolves named **Skoll** and **Hati.**

During Ragnarök, Hel sails a ship called **Naglfar** carrying all the dead to battle the Scandinavian gods. The ship is made solely from the fingernails of the dead!

ODIN IS KILLED BY FENRIR,

a giant wolf who is the son of the trickster god, Loki, in their final battle during Ragnarök.

91

At the end of
Ragnarök, only two
humans survive, named
LIF and **LIFTHRASIR**. They
climb a giant tree called
YGGDRASIL as the rest
of Midgard sinks into
a boiling sea.

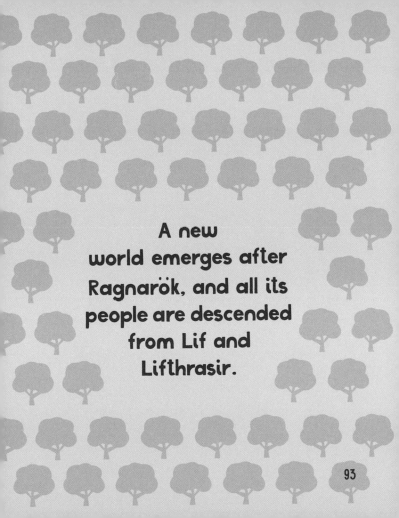

A new
world emerges after
Ragnarök, and all its
people are descended
from Lif and
Lifthrasir.

93

Myths from Asia and Oceania

The **Epic of Gilgamesh** is one of the oldest surviving written myths in the world.

The myth is from **Mesopotamia**, the area that is now Iraq, Kuwait, Turkey, and Syria. It tells how the gods created the wild man **Enkidu** to overthrow Gilgamesh, a tyrannical king of Uruk.

After defeating him in combat, Gilgamesh forms a friendship with Enkidu. Eventually, the gods kill Enkidu, and Gilgamesh roams the lands, grieving for his friend and trying to find a way to live forever.

IN JAPANESE MYTHOLOGY, THERE ARE SEVEN GODS OF LUCK.

The most important is **Benten**, who defeated evil dragons and is also the goddess of wealth, music, and learning.

The mythical land of the dead in Japan was called **Yomi**. A judge named **Emma-O** decided if someone had lived a bad life, in which case they had to wear a plaque around their neck listing all their sins.

In Japanese myth, after the gods finished creating animals, they made the **BAKU** from spare parts they had left over. These strange creatures brought good luck and were thought to eat up people's nightmares.

KINTARO,
meaning **GOLDEN BOY**,
was a legendary human hero in Japan
who possessed amazing strength.
This allowed him to defeat terrible foes,
including a **GIGANTIC SPIDER**
named **TSUCHIGUMO**.

After he caused trouble
on Earth, the Chinese gods forced
SUN WUKONG, THE MONKEY KING,
to work for them as a gardener.

❦

BUT THE MISCHIEVOUS
SUN WUKONG ATE PEACHES
THAT MADE HIM IMMORTAL AND
ESCAPED BACK TO EARTH.

For eating the peaches, the gods locked Sun Wukong inside a mountain for 500 years.

The **Leviathan**
is a many-headed sea monster from Mesopotamian myth.

It is mentioned in the Hebrew and Christian Bibles as an enormous sea serpent.

THE THREE GODS OF HAPPINESS IN CHINESE MYTHOLOGY ARE:

FU XING
GOD OF GOOD FORTUNE

SHOU XING
GOD OF LONG LIFE

LU XING
GOD OF WEALTH AND STATUS

IN CHINESE MYTHOLOGY, THE "FOUR PERILS" ARE FOUR EVIL CREATURES THAT CAN CAUSE HARM. THEY ARE:

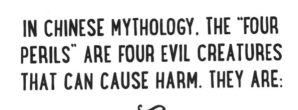

Hundun—a four-winged creature of chaos with six legs but no face

Qiong Qi—a winged tiger that eats people and starts wars

Taotie—a greedy sheep with a human face and tiger's teeth that eats or destroys anything in its way

Taowu—a squat bird with six legs that represents ignorance.

In Hindu mythology, **HANUMAN** is a monkey god who commands a monkey army devoted to **LORD RAMA**.

In one quest, Hanuman and his army build a bridge over a sea using magical floating stones so that Rama can rescue his wife, **SITA**, from an evil king named **RAVANA**.

In the Solomon Islands, people feared
a giant demon pig named

BONGURU

that had plants growing from its
back and a swarm of hornets
buzzing around its head.

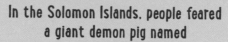

Bonguru led a herd of wild pigs that
trampled through villages and gored
anyone in their path.

110

The
YETI
is a
creature
from Nepal's
folklore said to be a
giant ape-like being
that lives high in
the Himalaya
mountains. Some
peoples in the
past worshipped
it as a god of
hunting.

ACCORDING TO ONE CHINESE MYTH,
AFTER A GREAT FLOOD BEGAN THE WORLD,

the goddess **NU GUA** was lonely,

so she fashioned the first people out of mud.

A nine-headed snake named

XIANGLIU

was said to bring **floods**
and **destruction** in Chinese
myths. In some versions of
the story, the snake's nine heads
all have human faces.

People in Papua New Guinea feared
attack from a giant people-eating
giant named **Malaveyovo**.

They left out their best fruit
and vegetables for the giant,
hoping he would just
eat these instead.

According to New Zealand myth,
a constant struggle continues between
TANE, god of the trees, and **TANGAROA**,
god of the sea.

Tahitian mythology tells of
a monstrous giant clam named

PUA TU TAHI

that lives in the
deep ocean.

THE ADARO IS A
PART-MAN, PART-FISH
SPIRIT from Polynesian mythology.
He has fish fins for feet, has a giant
swordfish spear growing out of
his head, and fires deadly flying
fish at his enemies.

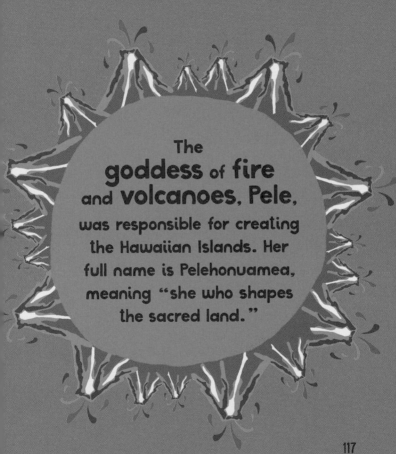

The **goddess** of **fire** and **volcanoes**, Pele, was responsible for creating the Hawaiian Islands. Her full name is Pelehonuamea, meaning "she who shapes the sacred land."

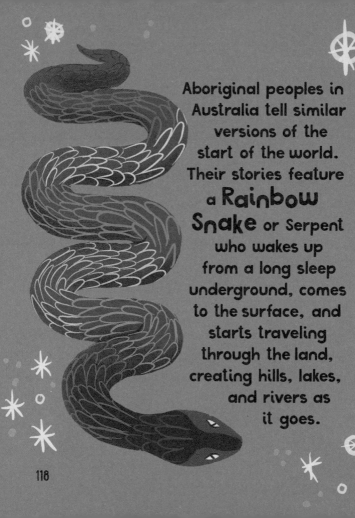

Aboriginal peoples in Australia tell similar versions of the start of the world. Their stories feature a **Rainbow Snake** or Serpent who wakes up from a long sleep underground, comes to the surface, and starts traveling through the land, creating hills, lakes, and rivers as it goes.

In Aboriginal mythology,
the Wawilak or Wagilag
Sisters were swallowed
by the Rainbow Snake
but managed to escape
from its stomach
and went on their way
creating and naming animals.

Myths
from the
Americas

Sightings of a large **ape-like creature** have been reported in North American forests for centuries.

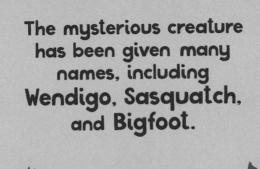

The mysterious creature has been given many names, including Wendigo, Sasquatch, and Bigfoot.

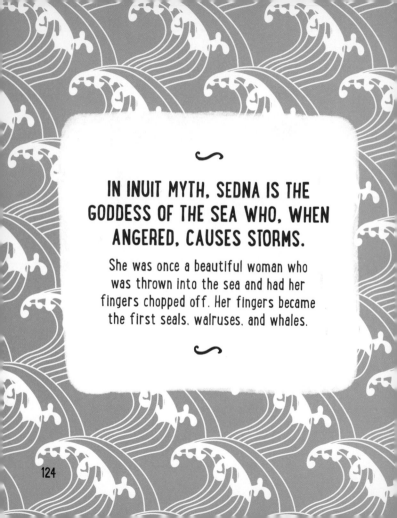

IN INUIT MYTH, SEDNA IS THE GODDESS OF THE SEA WHO, WHEN ANGERED, CAUSES STORMS.

She was once a beautiful woman who was thrown into the sea and had her fingers chopped off. Her fingers became the first seals, walruses, and whales.

In Inuit myth, QALUPALIK are human-like creatures with scaly skin, webbed hands, and fins. They steal children and either eat them or imprison them in a cave.

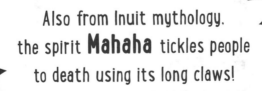

Also from Inuit mythology, the spirit **Mahaha** tickles people to death using its long claws!

125

In some native North American myths, Earth is supported on the back of a giant turtle.

The **Iroquois** peoples, for example, call the turtle **Hahnowa**.

Iroquois
mythology tells of a hungry
spirit called the FLYING HEAD—
a hairy human head with fangs
in its giant mouth that would
whiz around eating people.

◡

The Navajo of the American Southwest tell that the world first existed as **black with four corners, each marked by a different-colored cloud.**

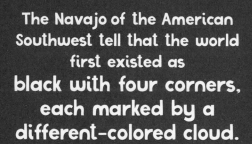

The blue and yellow clouds merged to form the first woman, and the black and white clouds formed the first man.

In **Navajo** mythology, the Milky Way was created by **Coyote**, a trickster god who grew impatient with the Black God carefully placing each star in the sky. Coyote threw the bag of stars all into the sky at once, creating our galaxy.

In **HOPI** mythology,
the universe began with
just two figures—**SPIDER WOMAN**
(also known as Grandmother
Spider), who was the Earth
goddess, and **TAWA**, the Sun god.

∽

Spider Woman led the first creatures on
Earth through a series of worlds where
the creatures transformed from unhappy
insects into happy, healthy humans.

In the mythology of the ancient MAYAN civilization of Central America, everyone who died traveled to XIBALBA—the Place of Fear. It contained nine levels, and rivers flowing with blood. The dead people were given tests, and if they passed, went to live in the sky in a much happier place than Xibalba.

Many of the temples and pyramids the Maya built had nine levels or nine columns to represent the nine levels of Xibalba.

THE **MAYA** HAD MANY DIFFERENT GODS. HERE ARE SOME OF THEM:

Acat–god of tattooing

Ah Muzen Cab–god of bees and honey

Ah Puch–god of death

Chaac–the god of rain and storms

Ix Chel–goddess of the Moon, harvests, and pregnancy

Yumil Kaxob–god of flowers and plants

THE **INCAS** OF
SOUTH AMERICA BELIEVED THAT
KON-TIKI VIRACOCHA
CREATED PEOPLE FROM PEBBLES
FOUND IN LAKE TITICACA,
BETWEEN THE MODERN-DAY
COUNTRIES OF PERU
AND BOLIVIA. HE DISGUISED
HIMSELF AS A HUMAN BEGGAR
TO MINGLE WITH PEOPLE AND
TEACH THEM HOW TO LIVE WELL.

The
SUN GOD, INTI,
was the most
important god for
the **INCAS.**

Inti's
sister
was the
**MOON
GODDESS,
MAMA-
KILYA.**

135

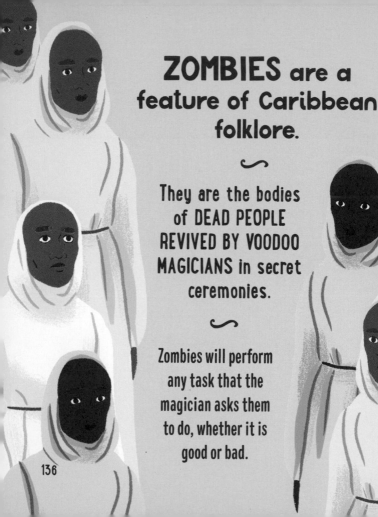

ZOMBIES are a feature of Caribbean folklore.

They are the bodies of DEAD PEOPLE REVIVED BY VOODOO MAGICIANS in secret ceremonies.

Zombies will perform any task that the magician asks them to do, whether it is good or bad.

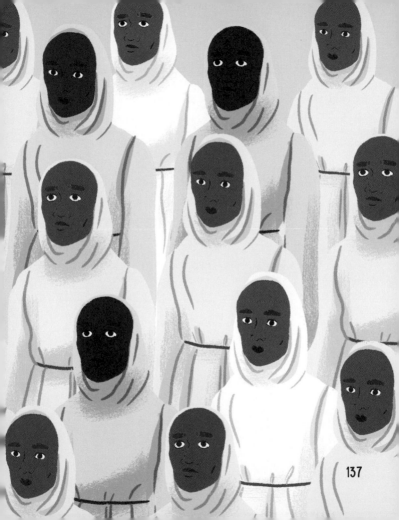

137

QUETZALCOATL

WAS A FEATHERED SERPENT AND
THE AZTEC GOD OF KNOWLEDGE,
WINDS, AND RAIN.

∽

He was said to have traveled
into the underworld to retrieve bones,
which he sprinkled with his own blood
to make the first people.

HUITZILOPOCHTLI WAS THE AZTEC SUN AND WAR GOD.

Tlaloc
was the
Aztec rain god.

He was said to have
four palaces, each housing a giant
container of water. The water was ferried
to Earth as rain by cloud servants
called TLALOQUES.

each time lit up by a new sun. **The Aztecs** believed that the world had been destroyed and re-created four times,

In Brazilian folklore, **CURUPIRA** protected forest creatures from hunters and poachers.

This character with bright red or orange hair...

...has backward-facing feet.

His footprints mislead hunters.

A scary creature in Brazilian folklore is a **HEADLESS MULE** named **MULA SEM CABEÇA** that spits fire from its neck.

MANY **MYTHS** AND **LEGENDS** HAVE BEEN TOLD FOR THOUSANDS OF YEARS.

~

They are such **EXCITING** stories that people still tell them today, and many have been turned into movies and plays.